Victoria

CALLING CARDS

Victoria

CALLING CARDS

CREATING BEAUTIFUL BUSINESS AND CALLING CARDS

HEARST BOOKS
New York

Recognizing the importance of preserving what has been written, it is the policy of William Morrow and Company, Inc., and its imprints and affiliates to have the books it publishes printed in acid-free paper, and we exert our best efforts to that end.

ISBN 0-688-11400-8
Library of Congress 91-42983

Printed in Singapore
First U.S. Edition
1 2 3 4 5 6 7 8 9 10

For *Victoria* —
Nancy Lindemeyer, Editor
Bryan E. McCay, Art Director
John Mack Carter, Director, Magazine Development

Edited by Alice Wong
Design by Barbara Scott-Goodman
Text by Shannon Rothenberger

Produced by Smallwood and Stewart, Inc.
New York City

Contents

FOREWORD

When one thinks about it, a calling card is really an illustrated story. It is always exciting to discover the person who has chosen this small nineteenth-century way of introducing him or herself to the world. Dollmakers, gardeners, designers, caterers, printers — the list of services represented by the calling cards we receive at *Victoria* magazine seems endless. Some are so special, it is difficult to part with them, and little collections of calling cards find themselves tucked into our lives, much like the cards found on an entryway tray when guests called generations ago.

Today's calling card is a perfect marriage between Victorian nicety and contemporary necessity. What better way to advertise than this most personal reminder of one's style and one's wares or services? As you meander through our book of calling cards, you will meet in a most delightful way many callers, not unlike those who long ago left cards in silver trays. We hope you enjoy the visit.

Nancy Lindemeyer

Editor, *Victoria*

INTRODUCTION

In these times of insistent advertisement, the gracious reserve of a simple calling card is a gentle reminder of one's presence, and the care poured into a finely crafted card is a welcome courtesy. A handsome calling card conveys an ability to inform, amuse, and please friends and clients; it is designed to be an intriguing balance of information and ornament. Quite an accomplishment in a small space! A bit like the poet, a calling card designer must remove every unnecessary word so that the remaining phrases will sing.

To begin, antique cards, really marvels of a bygone society, provide valuable inspiration for today's card designers. Their inventive use of calligraphy and embellishment is superbly valid today. In fact, many of the outstanding modern cards in this collection have incorporated such vivid notes of nineteenth-century elegance, from fanciful ornaments to rich monograms. These clever cards prove that a business card need never be dull or predictable.

All the cards in this festive collection, whether cherished ephemera or of more recent design, have their own unique charms. Each is valued for its elegant, humorous, or artistic qualities. The pleasure of receiving such a card is surpassed only by the joy of offering it.

William H. Wills
Henry C. Miller
Wm. G Sandler
Lizzie Stetzer

A DELICATE TRADITION

Imagine the joy of returning home to a hall table full of calling cards that have been left in a silver card receiver by thoughtful visitors. In a time of gentle manners and formal introductions, the exchange of calling cards was *de rigueur* socially, and played an essential role in developing friendships. It was customary to drop one's card at the homes of new neighbors, and to leave one for the hosts of balls, private recitals, and dinners on the day after the event. Leaving cards for one another was as meaningful as personal visits between acquaintances.

Like so many fashionable mores, the elegant custom of calling cards had its beginnings in France. By the end of the eighteenth century the practice had spread throughout Europe and was popular in America. Handmade cards were inscribed with the bearer's name, a greeting, and a spot of ornamentation. More elaborate cards were embellished with the romantic detailing of hand-painted vines, flowers, and fruits, or collaged with paper lace. By the mid-nineteenth century, printers were offering calling cards designed to order. In a printer's sample book one could choose from ten to fifteen styles of calligraphy, and when it was made possible by chromolithography, an assortment of colorful images.

As befitted beautiful cards, finely crafted card cases became popular accessories. Rare was the lady or gentleman without a dainty case to hold little gems of greetings. As status-enhancing items, the cases were themselves often elaborate and complicated in design. Together with the sweet tokens of affection they once held, these cases have now become treasured keepsakes.

The following pages present authentic calling cards and cases that have survived the romantic era in which they were created. From the exquisitely designed to the elaborately ornamented, they are samples of the timeless beauty of calling cards. Generations later, they continue to convey their creators' finer sentiments. In their loveliness, these antique cards and cases inspire us to participate in a delicate tradition.

Elegant, engraved calling cards were obtained from either a printer or calligrapher. Professional penmen placed elaborate displays in newspapers such as the *London Times* and the *New York Sun*. They advertised fine-line embellished cards with calligraphed names, greetings, and detailed landscapes.

In villages too small to support even a newspaper or printer, traveling penmen would set up shop on the village green. In the early days of literacy — when many could read but few could write well — calligraphers sat in town squares and wrote letters for hire. A penman would demonstrate, or have on hand, different samples of script style for letters and name cards. Sometimes his own card would be a painterly chromolithograph, reflecting the fine cards he personalized with a swirl.

Among the most splendid offerings were flourished cards. Inspired by baroque decorated initials, flourishing was the special ornamentation of skilled penmen. When flourishing, the pen was held still while the card was rotated beneath, creating the fine hatched swirls which distinguished the style. Certain calligraphers were famous for different styles of flourishing, and the dove and feather motifs were the hallmarks of experts. Examples of original flourishing work are highly valued today.

New Pocket Sample Folder No. 1.
FROM
RAY CARD COMPANY,
North Haven, Conn.

We have the Finest Goods, Latest Styles at Lowest Prices and the best Premiums. Our Printing is Neatly and Carefully done. Satisfaction guaranteed. ☞Every Pack shall be like the samples. ☞NO HALF PACKS PRINTED. Order all cards by number.

Card No. 95. With name, 12 for 10 cents.

Card No. 269. With name, 12 for 15 cents.

With the invention of a wax-resist color printing method known as chromolithography, bright batches of many-hued cards were offered by printers. A packet of a hundred cards could be bought for a dollar or two, depending on the style one chose from a printer's sample book. Chromos, as they were known, could be printed in so many shades that they resembled fine watercolors. Among the fanciful images printed were lush bouquets of flowers, doves, graceful hands, slippers, cupids, and butterflies. On the more lavish cards, it took over a dozen steps to print all the colors. Taken even further, the colorful cards could also be embellished with embossing, stamped cuts, scalloped and gilded edges, or dainty pierced work done with a razor. Only the bearer's name needed to be added; this might be written either by hand or printed in a variety of typestyles.

One popular and playful type of card was the hidden-name card. Cards were embossed and printed with images and greetings. The chromolithographs were then used to cover plain white cards that had been printed with a name. Recipients of hidden name cards had to lift the corner of the chromo to see the owner's name.

Early calling cards simply displayed the bearer's name in an elegant script, with perhaps a bit of ornamentation. Calligraphy was a rare and cherished skill, so it was no wonder that the man or woman possessing a signature like copperplate was much admired. Doves and flowers were among the favorite calling card images. The dove represented a "message carrier" and was often depicted with an envelope in its beak. Flowers and vines have a long history of decorating letters and provided lovely embellishments for cards.

Beautiful calling cards gave rise to new visiting customs. If a visitor happened by and it was not the family's "at home" day, the call could still be announced by leaving a card with the servant. According to Warne's *Etiquette for Gentleman* (1866), individual cards were to be left for the lady and for the master of the house. If there were sisters or daughters, cards were to be left for the young ladies as well.

Special ways of folding a card's corners sent discreet signals. If the top-left corner was folded down, it meant the caller came in person; an unfolded card meant a servant was sent. A folded top-right corner betokened congratulations and the lower-right fold, sympathy. If the lower-left corner of a card was folded, it meant that the visitor was leaving town on a journey of more than a few months' duration. A card left for a certain special person was folded in half diagonally, but if the visitor had wished to see the entire family, the card was folded in half like a book.

During the height of calling-card visiting, special emblems were pasted or printed on the back corners of cards, so that when a corner was folded a new little design appeared. From the 1840s to the 1930s, various customs for folding corners fell in and out of fashion. By the 1920s, the folding of corners was considered passé.

Amid Victorian propriety, gentlemen had precious little opportunity to make a young lady's acquaintance. Certainly, a gentleman was free to call on the lady of the house, to inquire after the health of the family, and to try to catch a glimpse of a special daughter of the household. But if the mother was not at home, the caller could only leave his card, as it was quite improper for a young lady to receive gentlemen callers.

Calling cards were a way to convey secret sentiments and private responses in chaperoned socials. Coded images and the language of flowers were used to send messages and gauge intentions without interference. Flower symbology imparted different meanings to calling cards. There were fifteen different rose messages alone, and colors carried further connotations: for instance a pink rose meant friendship, a yellow rose – jealousy. A moss rose was a confession of love, while a maiden blush rose warned, "You will be found out!"

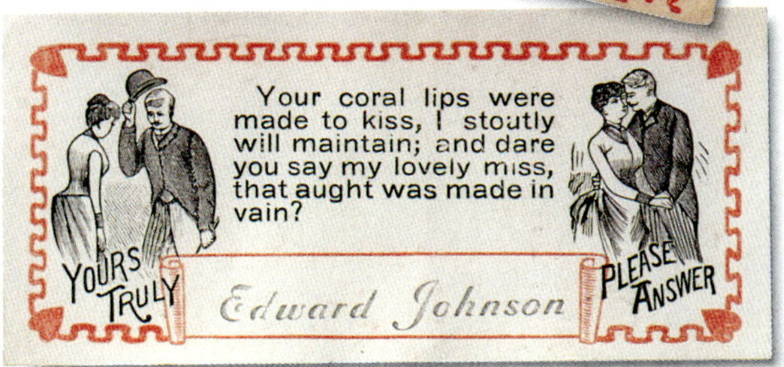

Openly flirtatious calling cards were known as "acquaintance cards." They were handed out by young men who waited outside after church or dances, hoping to escort a certain person home. They ranged from the innocent "May I see you home?" to bold requests for a kiss. If a young lady approved of a fellow, she would keep his card, and perhaps allow him to walk with her as far as her gate. If not, she might give him a card with a burdock flower for: "Touch me not!"

Charles K. Hoch

FORGET ME NOT

A fondness for discretion and suspense created many imaginative innovations such as cards with pasted-on envelopes that concealed tiny name cards. Such surprise cards seem a natural development from early calling cards, which were presented in plain envelopes. They were followed by "hidden name" cards, upon which the owner's name was obscured by a pretty colored flap pasted on the card. These embossed and scalloped calling cards with secret compartments approach sculptures in their design. The cards are like wonderful presents, containing layers of paper lace and hidden scenes that remain mysterious until they are opened by a delighted recipient.

If calling cards were an art, card cases were their luxurious frames. In fact, cases were more convenient for carrying cards than pocketbooks, and quickly became accoutrements of status. The slim rectangular holders were fashioned in countless styles and in a wealth of materials including sterling silver, mother of pearl, ivory, lacquer, horn, and wood. Most cases were of silver, such as these examples of silver filigree and pierced open work with mother of pearl. Valuable

tortoiseshell cases, like the diamond patterned example inlayed with mother of pearl, are rare finds, especially if they are in pristine condition. Vintage cases can be discovered at flea markets (as well as antiques shops and jewelers), and it is pleasant to know that price is not necessarily an indication of value. It is better to buy for taste; look for cases of unusual design which make best use of their materials, and are most evocative of the period.

Inspired by an old print, Paul Bott's calling card reflects his fondness for all kinds of old-fashioned flowers. His first employee at Twigs flower design shop gave him the 1850s print of a young delivery boy for an Austrian hotel. Because the boy is the image of sheer enthusiasm, Bott immediately wanted the print for his logo: "There's no hidden agenda. He's just *there*." The placement of large type giving only the shop's name on the cover of the inviting little book-folded card balances the image nicely. A green border strengthens the relationship between the two elements. Green from the print is picked up in the name and carried into the design inside.

Trim: 2 3/8 by 4 inches   Stock: smooth text, cream
Type: Bodoni Antiqua Condensed   Printing: 4-color process and green   Finish: book fold

FLOWERS
·
FÊTES
·
FESTIVALS

Twigs, Inc.
381 Bleeker Street New York, NY 10014
212 620 8188
3 World Financial Center New York, NY 10281
212 385 2660

A PORTFOLIO OF CALLING CARDS

Calling cards, whether for elegant social exchange — no more fumbling for a pen! — or as gift enclosures announcing a cottage business, are experiencing a revival. A distinguished calling card is not only a reflection of a business but of the owner as well. It is so much more intimate than the usual barrage of advertising, carrying its very personal message to people not yet met and remaining behind when its bearer is not present. A good card reflects the identity and quality of a secure enterprise; if a craftswoman loves her work, it will be evident from her card. Imaginative cards showcase the spirited character of small-business entrepreneurs and reflect the individual attention and personal service unavailable from large companies.

What sort of impression should an owner want to make? Perhaps the lacy florals of yesteryear would be lovely for social calls, but what's really needed is a design that uniquely expresses a profession or a particular craft. The goal is to leave a client with a favorable impression of the bearer's taste as well as a clear idea of exactly what he or she does. Dollmakers, decorators, caterers, and merchants all want their special talents to be remembered.

A calling card is a natural display for one's creativity, a kind of miniature portfolio of skill or a subtle swatch of style. A variety of different cards can be designed to match an owner's moods or tailored to clients' needs. In the following pages artists and designers such as Judith Cheng, Mary Polityka Bush, and Marna Balin each show how they use their cards as canvas to present, literally, original pieces of work.

An image on a calling card can speak eloquently of the business or craft it advertises. Cards for seamstresses Helen Lloyd and Holly Saunders simply use an illustration of a needle and of a seamline, while flower designer Andrea Stieff and garden landscaper Catherine Stimson choose images of women working in the garden to depict their craft. Cards for retail stores often carry images of the merchandise they sell, from books, sweaters, linens, and laces, to buttons, puppets, and dolls; these become silent reminders to shoppers.

The image that a business chooses to represent it does not always have to be literal. It can be very effective if it captures the feeling an owner wants his or her shop to have. Twigs chose the print of a delivery boy because of his sheer enthusiasm; Hudson Street Papers selected the photo of a young girl because of her mysterious femininity. An image can serve to reflect a mood, such as whimsy in cards for collectibles shops Michèle and The Hat & the Heart. It can also describe a style, such as the elegance in the cards for A Touch of Ivy, Forget-Me-Nots, and Tail of the Yak, each of which carries traditional merchandise.

A card's design should appeal to the type of customers it hopes to attract. The bold folksy taste of a patchwork-quilt lover is different from the sensibilities of a lace buyer. A painter's card aimed at local, private customers can be more idiosyncratic than one meant to impress large corporate accounts. A florist who specializes in weddings will have a more formal and sophisticated card than a business that caters to children — The Jenny Wren Press and Bunnies by the Bay, for example, wonderfully play up childhood sweetness on their cards.

Whether a card is meant to display a talent, skill, or product, or to express a mood or style, finding a perfect image is important. A wealth of design sources can be found in libraries, where fine art and design books containing centuries of reproduced mosaics, wood cuts, and tapestries from all over the world are available. Bookstores that carry vintage postcards and prints are other places to explore. Reproducing a piece of vintage art can help create a wonderful mood, but the art

Vintage fabric was the source for an all-over print on Ivy Weitzman's book-folded card. As she is a purveyor of fine textile-covered housewares, this design gives an impression of her taste. Printing the floral motif on a stock only a few tones lighter than the art gives the card a subdued appearance.

Trim: 2 by 3½ inches   Stock: smooth cover, cream   Type: Century Light Condensed   Printing: two colors: beige and gray   Finish: ribbon, book fold

must be researched for copyright restrictions. And copyright-free illustrations, which are printed in clip-art books, can have a predictable look. Perhaps the best solution is to create an original design by combining two or more decorative elements, or to choose a pattern that can be used for ornamental borders or delicate corners on plain calling cards. Sometimes an original illustration may be more appropriate for a particular business. Reviewing existing art can often be a means to inspiration that leads to unique results.

This process of choosing and creating art for calling cards is a special challenge, and it may take several tries to arrive at an image that both reveals the necessary information and looks handsome in a small space. This is not a simple task, but a flexible approach can make it more enjoyable. The following pages offer a portfolio of cards that illustrate how some enterprising people showcase themselves and their business.

Trim: 3½ by 2 inches
Stock: smooth card, white
Type: Baskerville Italic with Swash Caps and Baskerville Roman
Printing: one color: black
Finish: watercolor and ink

A calling card is a natural way for an artist to showcase a small sample of her work, and certainly easier than carrying a heavy portfolio everywhere she goes.

Judith Cheng shows how an ordinary letter-shop card can become exquisite with a bit of watercolor and a signature. The type and rules on her card are preprinted, but each card becomes unique by virtue of a different floral design. When the artist is not hand-painting flowers on furniture, pottery, or ceilings, she is customizing her calling cards while watching TV!

Instead of using a paintbrush, Mary Polityka Bush makes her mark as an artist with a needle. By stitching a yarn motif on a piece of punchwork, she eloquently demonstrates her specialty. Her cards are hand-embroidered in different techniques – cross-stitch, Swedish weaving, blackwork, or needlepoint – chosen to appeal most directly to the recipient of the card. A small card pasted on the perforated paper provides all necessary information.

Trim: 3½ by 2 inches
Stock: smooth card, white
Backing: punchwork
Type: Gill Caps
Printing: one color: green
Finish: needlework and hang string

Each of Marna Balin's calling cards is decorated with a different miniature drawing of the whimsical patterns she paints on walls. As an artist and product designer, she could not satisfy her creative spirit with a single image on all her business cards. Having a variety allows her to try out new work and keep her hand in shape. After a business meeting, she usually selects a card whose color and impression suit her client: "It's very rewarding to see how people delight in a hand-painted card!"

Trim: 3 by 3½ inches

Stock: smooth cover, white; speckletone cover, gray; smooth cover, natural

Type: Medici Script

Printing: one color: black

Finish: watercolor; occasional gold ink

These cards for an antiques shop and folk-art shop are as unique as the merchandise they purvey. Whimsical images in warm colors on odd-shaped cards convey the playfulness of the shops' owners.

Trim: 2¼ by 2¼ inches
Stock: laid cover, white
Type: Goudy Condensed
Printing: two colors: red and brown

Michèle's miniature square card has a memorable, neat, postage-stamp look. The owners chose to center their illustration of a cat as if he were staring out of a window framed by text. The smiling cat on a background of running mice was designed to match the sign outside the shop, where many cat items are sold. "We're very beastly," says owner Michèle Vigneux. Her husband, James Ronson, chose this format as a "break from the rectangular." Bold type is used to highlight the shop description without making the design too busy.

The tent-fold card for Hat & the Heart is of an unusually thin stock, with copy on the back. Ribbon rules create the illusion that the design continues beyond the paper, while playful type and art appear to float above a dot-patterned background. The art was inspired by an 1850 appliquéd crib quilt. The owners liked the image on the quilt because it does not define the type of store they have, nor does it ring masculine or feminine.

Trim: 2⅝ by 3 11/16

Stock: speckletone text weight; chipboard

Type: Signet Roundhand

Printing: two colors: black and red

Finish: tent fold

Garden spirits and fairies inspired these hand-watercolored cards for a dollmaker and puppeteer, respectively. Minimal copy on the front allows the art that each craftswoman chose to represent her creations to make a strong impression, while room for information on the back allows the cards to function as product tags as well.

Trim: 3 by 3 inches
Stock: smooth card, white
Type: Bauer Bodoni 1
Printing: one color: black
Finish: watercolor

The image on Denise Landriault's card evolved from a series of drawings she did about the garden pea, and reflects the fantasy and imagination that goes into her creations of hand-painted and sewn dolls. She named her card *Poupi La Poupée*, a term of endearment recalled from a childhood book about a doll, because of the sense of whimsy and sweetness it carries. The back of every card is inscribed with a little story about each doll before it is attached to the finished work.

As fairies receive the most delighted gasps from children at Sharon Brown's shows, she was pleased to find this copyright-free image from an antique rubber stamp to use on her card. As the cards often serve as tags for her puppets, there is space for a pricing sticker on the back.

Trim: 2 by 3½ inches
Stock: linen card, natural
Type: Nuptial script
Printing: one color: black
Finish: watercolor

Trim: 2 by 2¾ inches
Stock: recycled card
Type: hand-drawn
Printing: 4-color process
Finish: die-cut edges

Businesses that cater to children naturally want the fun and innocence of childhood to be reflected in their cards. Prints of original watercolors decorate these friendly calling cards for a plush-stuffed-animal company and a publisher of children's books.

Bunnies by the Bay — the bay is Fidalgo Bay in Anacortes, Washington — originally manufactured only stuffed bunnies, but expanded the menagerie to include cats and bears. The soft-colored card was designed to match the interior of their whimsically hand-painted shop. The extra-thick stock is die-cut with a wiggly edge for a warm, hand-felt appeal, and the miniature size fits comfortably in little hands.

A small watercolor of a little girl bending over to smell the flowers adorns a sweet card for The Jenny Wren Press, founded by Beth Mathers in honor of Tasha Tudor, the beloved children's author. It is a charming example of the lovely simplicity with which the artist has illustrated more than eighty books. Tasha Tudor is the oldest living woman illustrator of children's books in America, and the old-fashioned script typeface reflects to her country values and old-time ways.

Trim: 3½ by 2 inches
Stock: gloss card, white
Type: Snell Roundhand Script
Printing: 4-color process

Trim: 2 by 3½ inches

Stock: speckletone cover, beige

Type: Goudy Oldstyle and Goudy Bold

Printing: one color: burnt orange

These standard-size cards carry original illustrations that give a sense of what can be found in each of the stores they publicize.

Granny-Made's old-fashioned "Granny" silhouette with knitting needles in her hair was created to represent the store's woolies. A "sweatery" fiber-added stock was specially chosen to add a feeling of warmth. Granny Bert still knits baby caps for the shop owned by her grandson Michael, and her portrait was made by his brother Eric.

The owners of Renaissance Buttons wanted something playful on their card to show how enjoyable buttons could be. The festive jester juggling three buttons in the air, created by their designer, was the perfect image. Right after the owners began using this card, a customer presented them with a hand-sewn jester doll in a button-covered costume.

Trim: 2 by 3½ inches
Stock: felt cover, peach
Type: Souvenir
Printing: one color: green

Pulled Out a Plum's card is illustrated with a drawing of the designer's own thumb holding a plum aloft. The purple plum stands out charmingly against the black ink of the rest of the card. The nursery-rhyme-inspired logotype is fitting for a Victorian boutique, suggesting the possibility of rare finds within. "Plum" was also the childhood nickname given to owner Erin Williams-Morris by her mother.

Trim: 3½ by 2 inches
Stock: vellum cover, ivory
Type: Baskerville 2
Printing: two colors: black and violet

A background of tapestry florals has a nostalgic appeal appropriate for two stores that carry classic merchandise. The full-bleeds, or all-over motifs that seem to continue beyond the edge of a card contribute to a large-scale appearance.

Shirley Jensen's favorite flower, the forget-me-not, inspired her shop of flower-bedecked collectibles and fashions. The floral pattern sketched by her daughter Krista matches the botanical paintings she made for her mother's shop. The sweet stippling on the card recedes behind the florals and presses the white copy block forward. A thin rule frames the information and separates it from the background for clarity.

Trim: 3 1/8 by 3 1/8 inches
Stock: semigloss cover, cream
Type: Goudy Oldstyle, Snell Black Script
Printing: one color: blue

Tail of the Yak is a shop that offers a mélange of classic jewelry and accessories, many with floral motifs. Its card is made from a soft gray paper with a woven texture that emphasizes the tapestry effect of scattered sprigs of woodland foliage. This serene background offsets two bold copy shapes defined by a pink color block and a circular clip-art border. A bird sails above, representing the pair of doves that fly freely about the store named for the Tibetan symbol of good luck.

Trim: 2 3/8 by 4 5/8 inches

Stock: speckletone, frost white

Type: Goudy Open Face and Snell

Printing: two colors: black and pink

Trim: 4¼ by 2⅞ inches
Stock: laid cover, white
Type: Goudy Oldstyle and Goudy Bold Italic
Printing: one color: black

The rococo-style swash of tapestry is a lyrical example of the fresh- and dried-flower arrangements Pentimento creates. The sisters who own the shop chose an oversize card to represent their lavish arrangements, which resemble sixteenth-century floral paintings and incorporate fruit, berries, and tapestry. They also prove that cards for business partners need not be identical. The separate cards reflect creative individuality, yet still

maintain a business identity through the use of common elements such as fragments of the same tapestry and similar type. The floral art on each is particularly suited to the direction of the design, whether vertical or horizontal, and the blocks of copy cleverly correspond to its inward curves. Because the art is opulent, the type is treated with restraint.

Trim: 2 7/8 by 4 1/4 inches
Stock: laid cover, white
Type: Goudy Oldstyle and Goudy Bold Italic
Printing: one color: black

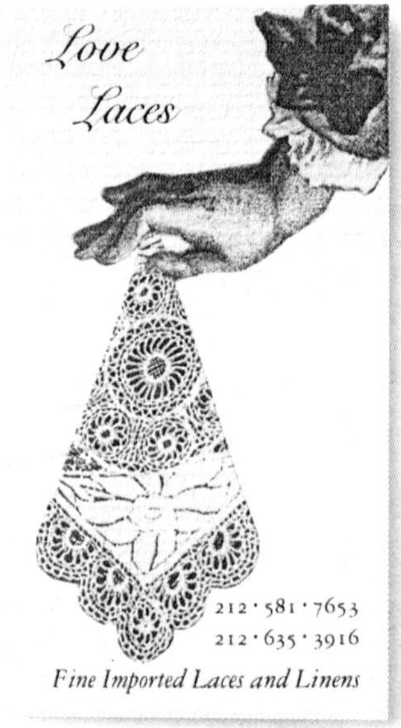

Actual lace and quilting patterns decorate calling cards for these purveyors of laces and linens.

Trim: 2 by 3½ inches
Stock: laid cover, pink
Type: Garamond ITC, Snell Roundhand
Printing: one color: black

Love Laces's collage made from an old postcard and a photocopy of a piece of antique lace was inspired by a Victorian design. Owner Mary Deegan is fascinated by the hand motif used on so many Victorian calling cards and she wanted an illustration in keeping with the delicate products she sells.

The rosy ink ridges of Piccadilly's ruled trapunto feel "quilted" to the fingertips, and the border embossed with fleurs-de-lys is reminiscent of scalloped bedding ruffles. An address is inscribed on the back of the folded card.

Trim: 3½ by 2 inches
Stock: wove text, white
Type: Signet Roundhand and Microstile Extended
Printing: one color: pink
Finish: embossed; tent fold

At first, Melissa Plummer of Plumelle at Plumquin wanted to use a piece of fine old lace on her card, but she discovered that the lace that worked best graphically was the edge of a simple crocheted doily. She bartered with her designer: a card in exchange for bed linens!

Trim: 3½ by 2 inches
Stock: glossy card, white
Type: Eras
Printing: one color: pink

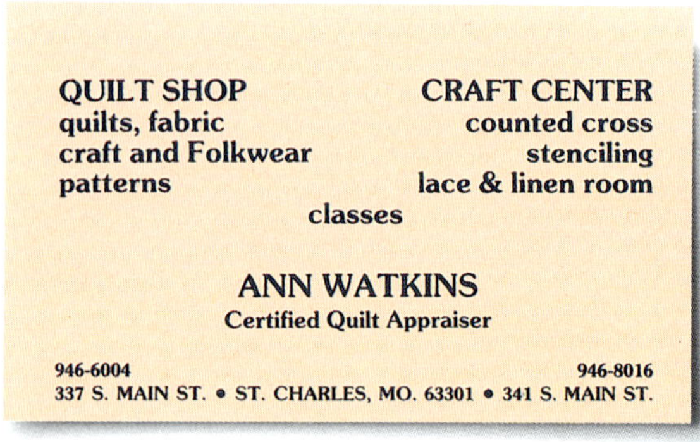

Images of the sewing trade, whether fabric, needle, or stitches, call attention to these cards for seamstresses.

A quilt-block illustration with an appliqué-look floral border suitably advertises Patches etc. quilt and needlework shop and craft center. Tilting the block on a corner provides eye-catching contrast within the rectangle of the card. The top flap of the card falls short enough to reveal the telephone numbers and addresses of the two shop locations, while keeping the card within the confines of standard business size. More information is available inside, where it doesn't detract from the design.

Trim: 3½ by 2 inches
Stock: vellum cover, beige
Type: Souvenir
Printing: two colors: red and blue
Finish: short-fold horizontal

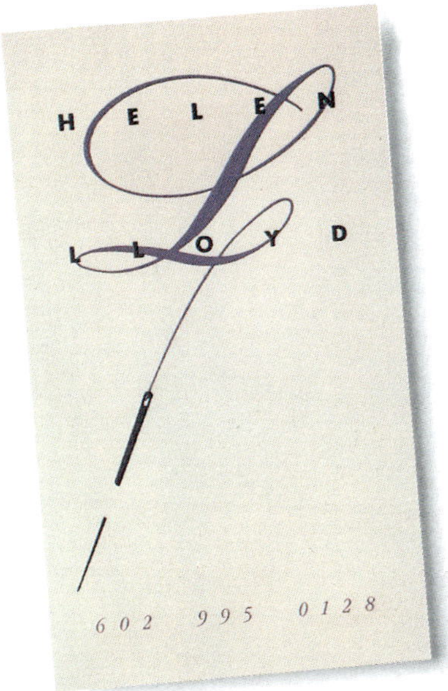

An illustrated needle and thread cuts a sweeping angle from corner to corner on Helen Lloyd's card. The thread forms a graceful capital *L* and the needle gives the illusion of piercing the card itself, imaginatively transforming the paper into crisp white linen. The dressmaker's son, Douglas Lloyd, omitted the address so as not to clutter his simple, elegant design.

Trim: 2 by 3½ inches
Stock: vellum card, off-white
Type: Futura Bold, Garamond Italic
Printing: two colors: lilac and gray

The fabriclike, fiber-added card for Seams To Be is edged by a "pinking" motif. Brightly printed stitches between the business name and telephone number complete the clues to Holly Wilson Saunders's profession. A simple typeface makes the small, light yellow type more legible, and an ornate capital *S* anchors the many little elements on her card.

Trim: 3½ by 2 inches
Stock: linen cover, cream
Type: University Light, Helvetica Bold, and Helvetica Medium Condensed
Printing: two colors: pink and yellow

A flower designer and a garden landscaper both use antique engravings that romantically depict women at their crafts to represent their own work.

Trim: 4 by 2½ inches
Stock: smooth cover, ivory
Type: hand-lettered
Printing: one color: gray
Finish: tent fold

Wildflowers' place-card–like, tent-fold design features an illustration of a flower gatherer from *The Girl's Own Annual VIII, 1886–1887*. The art conveys the free-form approach of Andrea Stieff, who does floral arrangements for weddings.

Trim: 4¼ by 6½ inches
Stock: vellum card, peach
Type: Deepdene Italic
Printing: one color: black

Catherine Colwell Stimson found this 1930s engraving by Clare Leighton in a gardening book, *The Four Hedges*. The landscaper felt that the image expressed the combination of grace and strength a true gardener requires. The company name comes from her discovery that Colwell was the name of the largest gypsy — or "tinker" — family in Britain.

The Tinker's Daughter Landscaping
Catherine Colwell Stimson
P.O. Box S-3526
Carmel, CA 93921
(408) 624-0590

Trim: 5 1/2 by 2 3/4 inches
Stock: laid cover, ivory
Type: Times Roman
Printing: two colors: red and black

The creative transformation of precious antique photographs is the secret to the special charm of calling cards for a bookshop and a book, stationery, and gift store.

An old print of the Bouquiniste, the strip of booksellers on the riverbank La Quai along the Seine in Paris, was transformed into the illustration for Three Lives bookshop. As the shop expanded, new figures were added to the drawing. Bullets stretch the business name to align it with the art. Formal uppercase letters accentuate the sophistication of this bookmark-card.

The image of a young woman, discovered at a yard sale, is used on the card for Hudson Street Papers. The owners felt that the vintage photograph captured the feminine feeling of their store without stating its merchandise. Cropping the photograph was a happy accident that not only enhances the girl's mysterious expression, but makes the card appear much larger than standard size, as the viewer's eye "completes" the cut-off image.

Trim: 2 by 3½ inches
Stock: linen cover, lemon
Type: custom
Printing: three colors: maroon, plum, and green

Thomas Whitehill's one-of-a-kind calling cards are collaged on oak tag shipping labels with the original hole punches and hang strings left intact. The illustrator is fond of Japanese motifs and often incorporates three-dimensional objects into his cards. It's no wonder that they sometimes come to resemble the little boxed assemblages he creates. His name and address are stamped on the back of each card, where they can be clearly read without competing with the illustration.

Trim: 2½ by 4¾ inches *Stock: oak tag*
Finish: mixed-media collage

CREATING A CALLING CARD

Once it becomes clear that a plain business card from the photocopy shop around the corner will never do, the fun begins. Before settling on a design, it's a good idea to explore a number of possibilities, even if they seem wildly inappropriate or expensive; inspiration can strike when you least expect it. Cards exist from postage-stamp to placemat size, on white glossy card stock to colored, textured stock. Typography is an art in itself, and volumes containing what seems like limitless typefaces are available. Printing choices range from one-color renditions of line drawings to four-color printing of photography on one or both sides of a card. Some cards are embossed or die-cut into elaborate shapes and sculptural dimensions. Others include folds and ribbon ties to provide additional interest. Often in reviewing all the different options in trim, stock, type, printing, and finishes, a theme will reveal itself, and a direction will naturally follow.

Clearly, many special little elements add up to a successful card design, but is there a formula for success? Probably not, and a good thing, too; otherwise all calling cards would look alike. Idiosyncrasies of taste and style lead to unpredictable results, but there are a few ground rules to keep in mind, whether to be followed, reacted to, or wisely broken, in the endless dialog of design.

TRIM

The standard 3½ by 2 inches is usually sufficient for a bit of art and essential copy. Larger cards are more noticeable, but they can be inconvenient to store in wallets and card files. Postcard-size cards have the advantage of being instant mailers. Cards smaller than standard size are another possibility, but they should not be so small that they are easy to lose. Discuss different trim options and costs with your printer. Some sizes may require nonstandard presses and may be expensive.

STOCK

The most popular materials are card or cover stock, either coated or uncoated. Coated stock, which comes in dull, gloss, or matte finish, is best for sharp, clear printing of color images and photographs

Suzanne Rheinstein loves simple, old-fashioned flowers, especially white ones, and adores the romance of a night garden. She thus commissioned an artist to paint a moonlit hollyhock on a background of black. This image serves as the logo for her business's stationery and gift-wrap supplies, as well as its calling card. A photograph of the painting is printed as a label to set into an embossed, beveled rectangle on the card.

Trim: 2⅝ by 4¼ inches Stock: smooth cover, white Type: Caslon Openface Printing: card: one color: green; sticker: 4-color process Finish: embossed; beveled; sticker; book fold

(because ink dries on the surface of the card and is not absorbed). Because cards make a tactile as well as visual impression, texture is another important consideration. Uncoated stock comes in a variety of textures – antique, felt, laid, linen, vellum, or wove – which add subtle depth and dimension to a card and provide interesting surfaces to the touch. Recycled papers, also offer unique textures and colors, as well as a boon to the environment.

The other consideration in selection of a stock is color. White is the clearest background for dark type, but it can get dirty quickly. Black cards are striking, but show bends and creases easily. Gray and beige papers are softer and come in shades from dove to charcoal and cream to brown.

TYPE

An enormous world of typefaces exists, from formal Bodini to elegant Snell Roundhand to bold Franklin Gothic. A creative, original typeface can suggest an individual identity; an antique style may imply old-fashioned craftsmanship and values. The size of a typeface, and the format used, both contribute to the overall impression. A large, bold version of a typeface will be clearly distinguishable from a smaller, italic version. Varying the size and format of one typeface on a card can provide visual interest while maintaining consistency.

PRINTING

Though four-color printing often creates a strong image, it is more expensive, and is not always necessary to achieve dramatic effects. One- or two-color printing may be all that a simple line illustration requires. Another economical alternative is to add colors by hand after the type and the outline of art have already been printed in one color. And printing on the back of a card is a simple solution to any space problem. Two-sided printing costs more but can give a design twice the impact. The reverse side can be used to put a different spin on the graphics on the front. It can also allow a strong image on the front to be free of distractions from too much type.

SPECIAL FINISHES

Some card makers spend hours hand-painting or collaging their creations. Others pay for embossing, die-cuts, or other additions to make their cards stand out. A raffia or ribbon tie adds charm and allows a card to be attached to a package. A folded card with information inside has all the finesse of a private note, and the element of surprise when it is opened. It can also function as a product card, the extra space providing room for a description of a company and its merchandise.

While considering the different options available for each element in the creation of a card, it is important to keep in mind the need for legibility and balance. Too much color or type that is too ornate can be overwhelming on a small card. A detailed illustration printed in black will lose its appeal on a dark stock. When the type and the printing process are elaborate, a simple stock works best. If a special stock is chosen, allow it to be noticed and keep what is printed on it basic. Weigh the elements against one another and strive for a balance among the components. Trim, stock, type, printing, and finishes should complement, and not compete with, each other.

Remember that decisions made about calling cards are never irreversible: New cards can always be designed — in fact, that's half the fun. The cards featured in this section exemplify the many design processes. Each one is a sample of a personal odyssey in design that will inspire and delight.

Line drawings are simple to reproduce and make for attractive and economical calling cards.

Trim: 2⅛ by 3½ inches
Stock: glossy card, ivory
Type: Baskerville
Printing: one color: black

In the Angels Workshop card, a Dürer angel engraving represents the creative spirits involved in a children's wear shop. When an illustration is somewhat detailed, it is important that the copy blends — or at least does not compete — with the art. Here, it curves around the angel to create a logo, and beneath it, the use of italic type and upper-case letters in the same typeface provides unity and contrast in the design.

A simple black and cream card makes an impression with miniature line drawings of an illustrator's special subjects. Working from a photograph and a description of a personality, Wendy Christensen creates portraits of cats for private and commercial commissions. Each cat in the border faces the center of the card, drawing attention to the information. A double border makes the available space smaller, but frames an intimate landscape. Two blocks of simple sans serif type on each side balance the detailed art.

Trim: 3½ by 2 inches
Stock: smooth cover, cream
Type: Helios
Printing: one color: black

Cynthia Petters found this print of an angel painting a peony so long ago that she doesn't remember the source. She filed it away for years, not knowing that one day it would be perfect to represent the "Garden Angel" dolls she makes. Like the cherub on her card, she paints each doll with a verse chosen to fit any occasion. Minimal type in a small point size blends in color with the illustration and forms a "ground" for the angel to sit upon.

Trim: 3½ by 2 inches
Stock: recycled cover, cream white
Type: Garamond
Printing: one color: pink

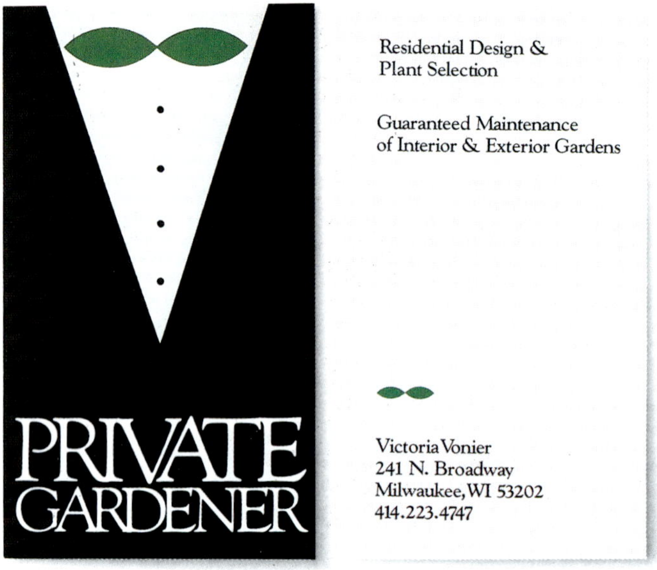

Cards make bold graphic statements when art and color are allowed to dominate and copy is kept to a minimum.

Private Gardener combines a butler's tuxedo and a leaf bow tie to play up the company name and represent the custom service it provides. The glossy stock is matte-coated on the jacket to prevent fingerprints from marring the black area. The white shirt remains shiny, to create a contrast in "fabrics." A business description, address, and phone number are printed on the back to allow the full-bleed image on the front full impact.

Trim: 2 by 3½ inches
Stock: glossy and matte card, white
Type: Goudy
Printing: two colors: black and green

The owners of Repeat Performance cater to costume designers who work on period films in Hollywood: "We wanted a card to reflect a classic period image in people's minds . . . in 'Technicolor!' " Because their illustrator worked with so many colors in tight registration (touching each other), he separated each color with a thin black line to avoid blurring. Using the logotype as the name on the storefront smoothly incorporates the copy with the nostalgic design.

Trim: 3½ by 2 inches
Stock: glossy card, white
Type: hand-lettered
Printing: 4-color process

A marvel of economy and dash, the Gael Paints card delivers a name, a description, and a logo in one stroke. A telephone number alone is sufficient, as this decorative interior painter conducts no business through the mail. The sans serif type in all upper-case letters blends with the paintbrush, and its placement so close to the art enhances the direct design.

Trim: 3½ by 2 inches
Stock: glossy card, white
Type: Eurostile Extended
Printing: 4-color process

Trim: 2 by 3½ inches
Stock: laid cover, sand
Type: Goudy Oldstyle
Printing: one color: red

Trim: 3½ by 2 inches
Stock: vellum cover, tan
Type: Engraver's Roman
Printing: two colors: black and red

A formal calling card features a neat logo and clear type. These standard-size, one- or two-color cards follow a basic formula and are effective in their simplicity.

The zinnia logo on the Petals card began life as a full-color gold-leaf sign painted on the window of the shop. After the design won a prize in an international competition, the florists used the image in print ads and, of course, on their calling card.

An awareness of design choices can make it even more challenging for a graphic artist to create her own card than to design for others. It took years for Patricia Melville to develop her card, but it was worth the wait, as she has achieved a handsome balance of rich color and strong type aligned with art. The designer wanted something striking that would not classify her by style or sex. She is pleased with her final choice of an antique woodcut in vermilion ink.

Sandy and George Green engaged a design team to create a distinctive period logo for their bed and breakfast, a restored 1865 inn. The vertical format for the Plumbush card allows the oval logo prominence, while open line spacing calls attention to the telephone number. Contrasting colors make for a vivid card, and reverse rules and type are necessary for readability on a dark background such as this one.

Trim: 2 by 3½ inches
Stock: laid cover, ivory
Type: English Times Group
Printing: two colors: green and plum

Trim: 2 3/8 by 4 inches
Stock: speckletone cover, cream
Type: Copperplate and Veljovic Medium Italic
Printing: two colors: purple and blue

Though these cards are not quite formal with their use of larger and more elaborate logos or decorative borders, they each maintain a classic appearance.

The designer of the Props card had created an enormous set of curtains for an outside wall of the theatrical gift and supply shop and had them made in fiberglass. They have become something of a local landmark and function as the store's "sign." His line-art illustration of one curtain serves well as a large logo on the store's business cards.

Elan's tiny sketch is a detail from the plans for Elizabeth Toel's fantasy garden. The image combines with the business name and description to form a two-color block of art and copy. The landscaper stamps the art and address on her card to decrease printing cost, and to allow for an easy change of address.

Trim: 2 by 3½ inches
Stock: laid cover, white
Type: Trojan Plain and Trojan Bold
Printing: one color: plum
Finish: rubber-stamped

For Pugh Design, the cornice of a classical Ionic column appropriately adorns its sophisticated calling card. The gold and deep teal of the logo are repeated on the top border of the card, for a note of understated elegance. Red and gold speckles subtly echo the art and thin red rules, and add warmth to the formal type treatment.

Trim: 2 by 3½ inches
Stock: laid cover, off-white
Type: Times
Printing: three colors: gold, burgundy, and deep teal

Witty type and strategic graphics can combine to create charming and original cards. In both of these clever cards, large, dramatic type is used to achieve very different effects.

Trim: 4 3/16 by 3 1/8 inches
Stock: smooth card, white
Type: hand-lettered
Printing: one color: black

On the Shoofly card, the illustrations of fanciful floating copy and merchandise reflect the name of this children's shoe store. The whimsical hat, belt, and shoe literally fly along with the type, as if caught in a cheerful gust of wind, and young children enjoy identifying the flying objects. The owner originally commissioned a Matisse-style illustration, but decided on more timeless imagery so she would never tire of looking at her card.

An ornate Victorian clip-art spoon and type drawn on a computer make for a unique combination in Savoy's fun design. Die cutting adds a dimension of fascination – this card demands to be touched! The design went through many stages – spoon and type were tried in various combinations. At one point all the letters were formed of vegetables – "too complicated!" said designers Salestrom and Zingg. They ate many a meal at Savoy before arriving at a design with the homey, warm feeling of the restaurant.

Trim: 3 1/16 by 2 1/8 inches
Stock: speckletone card, cypress
Type: Lithos Bold
Printing: one color: burnt red
Finish: die cut

Trim: 3½ by 2 inches
Stock: laid cover, tan
Type: Papyrus
Printing: two colors: moss green and brick red

Tag:
Trim: various
Stock: handmade paper
Finish: ribbon; sealing wax

Decorated initials have been used for over one thousand years, since eighth-century Celtic monks first embellished the pages of their *Book of Kells*. Today's fanciful initialers can find unlimited inspiration in the pages of typographical history, and one flourished initial can transform a formal calling card into a work of art.

On a handmade paper hangtag for Patina Millinery, the Victorian Tuscan-style initial *P* is pressed into green and gold sealing wax. A color scheme of moss green, brick, and taupe relates the elaborate hangtag to the relatively simple business card.

Emerald Forest Entertainment's *E* is historiated, or inhabited by an illustrated scene, in a tradition dating from Gothic times. The Oz lovers at this music publishing company decreed that their illustrator design a large *E* incorporating a tree and castle as a reference to the imaginary kingdom. The illustrator found inspiration for the character in an antiquarian book and chose green type on a speckled background to complete the fantasy.

Trim: 3½ by 2 inches
Stock: speckletone cover, cream
Type: Centaur and Arrighi
Printing: 4-color process and green

The arabesque *A* for Arcadia, with a classic vine motif, recalls the woodcut art of sixteenth-century France. Printed in two shades of blue against a sweet pink background, the letter block becomes a stronger area of interest.

Trim: 3½ by 2 inches
Stock: laid cover, pink
Type: Goudy
Printing: two colors: plum and blue

Trim: 3½ by 5½ inches
Stock: laid cover, white
Type: Goudy Oldstyle
Printing: one color: black

Larger calling cards can have enlarged possibilities. These two cards utilize the extra space to display antique engravings.

The Cats Cradle card is postcard-size, and is mailed to potential guests of this Bridgehampton inn. Sources for engravings abound and are usually copyright-free, from clip art and antiquarian books to collections such as *1800 Woodcuts by Thomas Bewick and His School*, where the perfect Cats Cradle cat was found.

Herbalist Kimberly Childers's card is large enough to show the little girl with a big watering can in full detail, and scored to fold to standard size for practical storage. Economical black-and-white printing is a simple and effective presentation for rich wood engravings.

Trim: 3½ by 4 inches
Stock: linen cover, white
Type: University Roman
Printing: one color: black
Finish: scored for tent fold

Black ink on white stock is a good medium for ornate illustrations, as fine lines can be printed with maximum clarity.

Trim: 5 1/16 by 3 7/8 inches
Stock: matte card, white
Type: Versailles
Printing: one color: black

The calling card for a London rare-print and antique-frame shop is bordered with a reproduction of a late-seventeenth-century engraving, representing many of the facets involved in art and print dealing and the subjects they deal in — botanical, animal, and architectural. Shading on the edge of the copy block creates the illusion of a plain calling card lying on a fanciful tray.

A detailed illustration by Alice Simpson is also best displayed in simple black on white. The artist frames her work inside a thin rule that doesn't distract from the type. The flowing lines of the calligraphy above the illustration and the address pull art and text together.

Type: 3 ½ by 5 ½ inches
Stock: smooth cover, white
Type: calligraphy and Bodoni
Printing: one color: black

Trim: 4⅞ by 3⅞ inches
Stock: smooth cover, pearl white
Type: Copperplate
Printing: one color: gray

These large, or European-size, calling cards are printed in gray ink. Gray type is dark enough to be read, yet is softer, friendlier, and can look more sophisticated than black type.

Product designer Janet McCaffery chose a nineteenth-century French wood engraving to create a wide, flowery frame for a neat octagon of type in the center of her card. A book of Victorian spot illustrations and ornaments was the source of this motif, to which the designer added a few sketched flowers. Formal, all-capital type provides a nice contrast to the delicate border.

The proprietor of Friends Hairdressing Salon, Phillip Kells Rimmer, requested an European-size card: "People say my card is an inconvenient size, but I'm not a very practical person." He asked that the cherubs on his card be holding scissors and a comb, and he enjoys the bows the designer Bob Thomas added to their ankles for a romantic feeling: "I like the overkill in romance. I like it overdone, not underdone." Details such as the shop's address appear on the back of the card.

Trim: $4\frac{7}{8}$ by $3\frac{3}{8}$ inches
Stock: smooth cover, off-white
Type: handscript
Printing: two colors: charcoal and rose

Generous white space can be a strong design element that displays simple art to its best advantage.

Trim: 5¼ by 3½ inches
Stock: smooth cover, white
Type: Baskerville Caps
Printing: two colors: black and blue
Finish: adhesive backing

On Jacqui Morgan's card, open space is informally balanced by three juicy brushstrokes that succintly convey the message that the illustrator uses watercolor exclusively. The cards are self-sticking, so they can be used as mailing labels, with plenty of room to add the receiver's address. Small upper-case letters running along the bottom of the card are easy to read, yet do not detract from the elegantly minimal design.

Bell'occhio's charming logo was inspired by old French schoolbook labels. The gift-shop owners liked the slightly shaky quality of hand-lettered type, finely presented on their card with plenty of white space. The arabesqued copy blends smoothly with flowing ornamental curves and with a tiny drawing of a hand inscribing in Latin, "Art is long, life is short."

Trim: 4 by 4 inches
Stock: smooth cover, white
Type: hand-lettered
Printing: one color: black

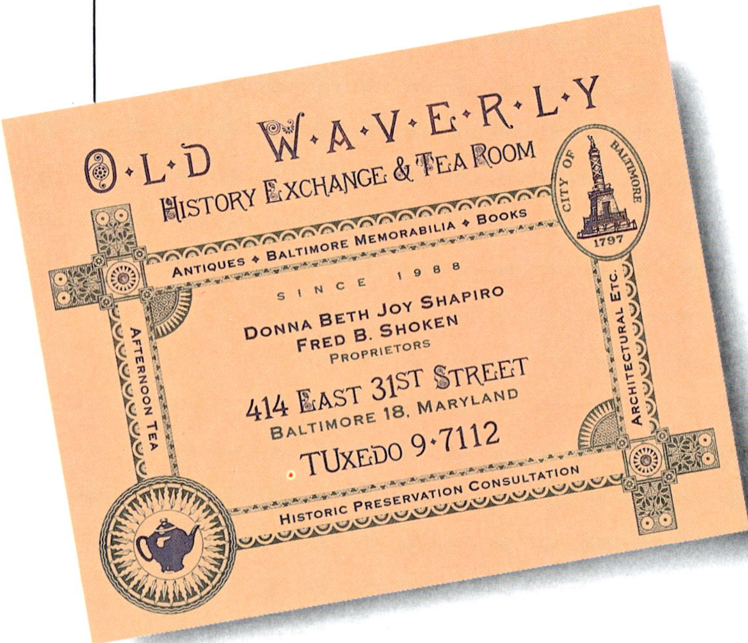

Trim: 4¼ by 3⅜ inches
Stock: laid cover, melon
Type: Aesthetic and Copperplate
Printing: two colors: violet and green

An old business-card adage states: "Keep the color in the ink, not in the paper." Two historically flavored designs on unusually colored stocks cheerfully, and successfully, break the mold.

In the Old Waverly card, alternating lines of violet and green Gothic type are displayed on melon-colored stock. Old wallpaper designs provide borders that cleverly incorporate art with copy about the history exchange and tea room.

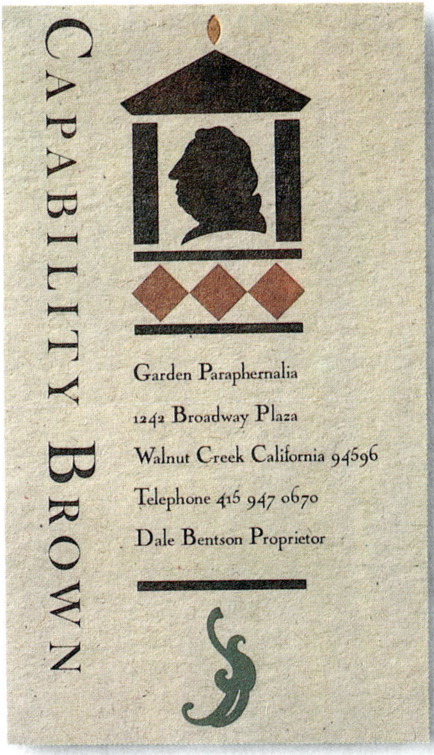

The card for Capability Brown – which is, naturally, brown – features a silhouette of the eighteenth-century British garden designer after whom the shop is named. A classic temple, always included in his gardens, frames the portrait. Unusually placed, the large type of the company's name provides a quirky balance for the copy.

Trim: 2¾ by 4¾ inches

Stock: speckletone cover, brown

Type: Baskerville and Cochin

Printing: three colors: black, terra-cotta, and green

Finish: foil stamping

Personal touches, no matter how simple, distinguish a calling card. These two cards are strengthened by a bit of handcoloring.

Trim: 3½ by 2 inches
Stock: felt cover, cream
Type: Papyrus
Printing: one color: black
Finish: hand-colored with colored pencil or watercolor

Ginny Joyner has her card printed in black ink with a design she created to show a small sample of her work. The floral swash underscores her name and gently narrows to make room for a phone number under her title. The illustration is then enhanced with some vivid color that she adds with pencils or watercolors. This process allows the illustrator to change colors instantly to achieve different moods, and to make her cards unique. Though she enjoys personalizing her cards, the illustrator also had a batch printed in color for convenience.

The card for a business named for a flower that grows in the Pacific Northwest was designed to express the owner's love of "a magical world from long ago." Kathryn Hettinga drew the decorated letter *T* in black and had the type set in Goudy Oldstyle, an elegant but simple type that does not conflict with the ornate capital. The cards are printed on recycled paper for a grainy handmade look, and hand-colored to emphasize the attention to small details the artist customarily gives to all her paintings.

Trim: 2 by 3 1/2 inches
Stock: recycled paper
Type: Goudy Oldstyle
Printing: one color: black
Finish: hand-colored with watercolor

Trim: 2½ by 4 inches
Stock: card: recycled paper; mount: handmade paper
Type: Zapf Calligraphy
Printing: card: one color: black; mount: varied
Finish: double ribbons; mounted

The creators of these cards combine an appreciation of fine ribbons – which offer an exciting range of colorful and textural embellishments – and an awareness of the environment.

The owners of Suzy's Searsport Boutique choose different-colored double baby ribbon ties imported from Germany to accentuate the colors of exuberantly hand-marbled card mounts. Conservation motivates their use of printer's leftover stock pieces for their gift-shop cards.

The colors of the French ribbons on the bookmark cards for Love Gifts vary according to the proprietors' whims. A recycled paper was chosen not only for its natural look and feel, but also because it is less wasteful. As the mother-daughter business team proclaims: "We are all ultimately responsible for the earth."

Trim: 2 by 6 inches

Stock: speckleone cover, cream

Type: Avant Garde Book

Printing: one color: black

Finish: French ribbon

Trim: 3½ by 2 inches
Stock: gloss card, white
Type: Caslon Book, Continental script and serif
Printing: 4-colors process
Finish: ribbon; hollow-cast key

Some cards are not merely ornamented, but become ornaments. Special finishings bring these cards into the realm of the sculptural. With ornate designs, type has to be treated carefully for readability, and must not make a card too busy.

Sindy Kelley orders the hollow, light metal alloy keys from a bead company for sixty cents apiece and ties them to her hole-punched cards with a violet ribbon. She chose type in a small point size, widely spaced, to keep her card clear. Reverse type in all caps is legible within her intricate logo.

The calling card for Buttons & Beyond also serves as a care label for the vintage buttons Paula Goldberg uses to embellish her clients' clothing. The circular wrapping paper photo-collage of beautiful old buttons and sewing paraphernalia itself resembles a large button. Four actual mother-of-pearl buttons are pasted on the card where the buttonholes would be, and the card is finished off with a golden cord. All printed information appears on the reverse of the card. As the type is very small, a clear sans serif face is important for readability.

Trim: 3 inches in diameter

Stock: wrapping paper on card

Type: Mistral

Printing: one color: black

Finish: buttons; thread

Trim: 2¾ by 4¼ inches
Stock: felt cover, peach
Type: Helvetica
Printing: one color: black
Finish: watercolor; raffia

Whether it involves hand coloring a card or adding on a slip of raffia, making a card exceptional can be a time-consuming effort that sometimes requires more than one pair of hands.

A raffia tie imparts rustic charm to Nancee McDonell's jewellike rendering of the tools of her trade, scattered along the diagonal axis of a rose. As this artist devotes much of her attention to her business of designing one-of-a-kind cards for stores, her mother helps out by punching the holes and tying the raffia to the cards.

Terra Cotta's card, printed on warm-toned, textured stock, is as earthy as its name suggests. The lovingly painted pear on each card, centered as a classic medallion, is the collaborative effort of several members of the owners' families — even a five-year-old niece. The raffia allows the card to function as a tag for packages from the garden and gift store.

Trim: 3 1/4 by 4 3/4 inches
Stock: linen cover, tan
Type: old metal Ludlow type, turn-of-the-century lettering
Printing: one color: brown
Finish: watercolor; raffia

WORKING WITH A DESIGNER

Designing your own calling card can be an overwhelming endeavor to take on in addition to running a business. If time is a consideration, if you don't feel ready to deal with color charts, point sizes, and paper samples, or if you would simply feel more comfortable working with a professional, hiring a graphic designer is a good option. Inquire of friends or call the local illustrators' or graphic artists' guild for a recommendation. Large design studios are listed in the telephone directory. Look through designers' portfolios to decide whose particular style is for you.

Once you have chosen a designer, it is important to communicate a clear idea of the feeling you want the card to have, even if you are not sure what imagery you would like. Do you want a whimsical, loose drawing or a strong, abstract logo? Should the art be a metaphor or an exact representation of your profession, or just an evocative allusion to your style? Some cards depict the tools of a trade or the exterior of a shop. Perhaps you want the copy to "say it all" with type rather than illustration. The designer should also become acquainted with your product and visit your shop, if possible. A good designer will try to get a feeling for your personality and the image you want for your business.

Mya Kramer of (?Paradox!) A Design Business in San Jose, California, believes that the best design work comes out of close communication and involvement between the client and designer – a true creative collaboration. After observing Dorothy Wilson Catering of Santa Cruz

In the first stage of designing a card for Dorothy Wilson Catering, (?Paradox!) presented their client with five ideas. Dorothy Wilson's responses told the designers what she did not want:

"Great for packaging!"

"Nice, but not us!"

Dorothy also rejected two all-type concepts with:

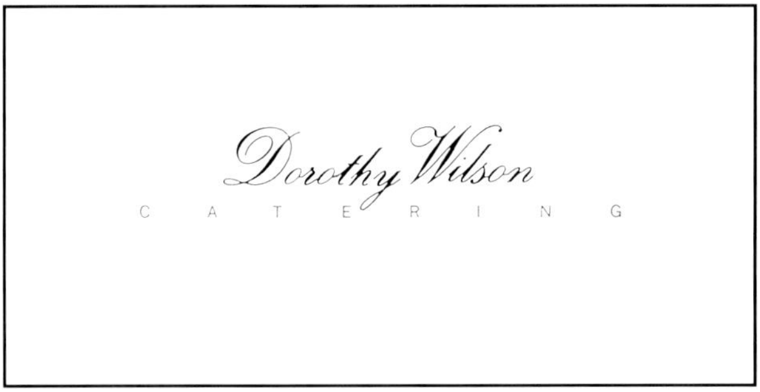

"Too formal!"

"Doesn't say enough about food."

at work, Mya noticed that Dorothy Wilson, besides being a good caterer, also finds perfectly suited and often very unusual locations for events; she then decorates the setting and the food to transform the look of the event to match her client's fantasy. The designers at (?Paradox!) began work on a series of illustrations in the styles of Piccasso and Matisse to reflect the artful presentation and vision they associate with the caterer. Further inspiration for the designs came out of conversations between Dorothy and Mya. "I tried to capture the timeless elegance so evident in the magic that Dorothy puts into her food presentation, and her events," said Mya Kramer.

The design selected went through several refinements until the final one was approved: a

A positive response and a specific suggestion from the caterer let the designers know they were on the right track:

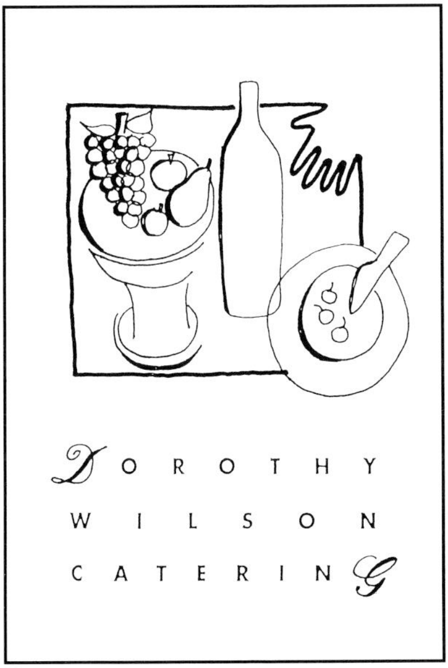

"Love the idea. Can we add elements of an event?"

"Let's develop this idea!"

three-color, vertical business card with plum-colored ink for the company address and telephone number informally balancing a loose-brush still life of columns, a place setting, a bottle of wine, and an urn of fruit in plum, deep teal, and olive green. Beneath the illustration is the calligraphic lettering of the company name in plum. The overall effect is of a mythical culinary outing. The rest of the company's design system includes embossed, woven-finish letterhead and printed packaging ribbon. Dorothy concluded, "When we held the final card in our hands, we knew that we ended up with something that not only described our image, but also enhanced it. We knew we had something that really told the world who we are."

The final stages were of developing a structure and refining elements for the right balance of formality and spontaneity:

"Nice feeling but no sense of place. Add architecture and loosen up letters."

"Can the window be something more formal?"

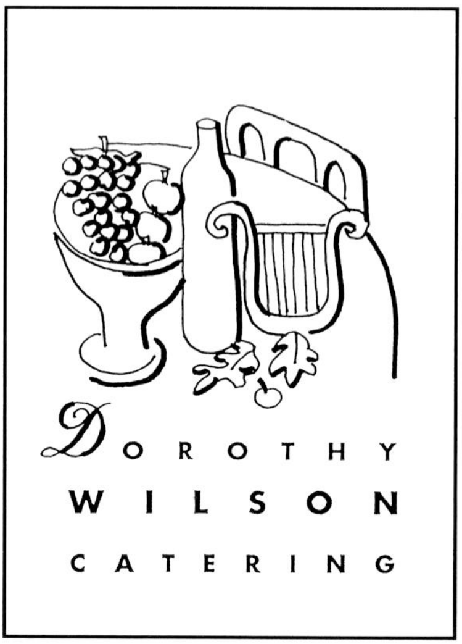

"Better, but it isn't quite it. Try another approach."

"Column too weak!"

Finally, the result of a creative collaboration:

"Great. That's it!"

Trim: 2 by 3½ inches

Stock: speckletone cover, cream

Type: Times Roman Italic and hand brush drawing

Printing: three colors: plum, olive green, and teal

WORKING WITH A COMPUTER

While working with sketches, mechanical boards, and a photocopy shop or printer is the traditional process of design and production, computers open up a world of possibilities in the creation of a calling card. Type, graphics, and even separations can be done with computers and the programs now available. A computer-designed card can quickly go through many changes on the screen, thereby allowing for increased flexibility and creativity.

Even basic word processing programs provide many typefaces with different sizes and formats. These simple programs, when teamed up with fine-quality laser printers, can provide type for print production. Graphic design programs allow the user to experiment with variations of a particular design or with a series of designs, as well as customizing type and adding artwork. Art may be scanned in by an outside service, or created directly onscreen using one of the many illustration programs. For those who are familiar with computer design technology but lack the necessary hardware, some service bureaus rent computer terminals on an hourly basis. Rental time is not inexpensive, so it is advisable to have a design roughed out ahead of time.

Though the entire design process can be done electronically, the computer can also serve as an additional tool for traditional methods. It can be used simply to get an idea for type size and placement, or to manipulate existing elements together. A simple self-design was enhanced by a computer scanning and manipulation program for Paula Arnt-Berger's trompe l'oeil painting business, A Gilded Vine. Paula started with pencil and paper to work out original art for her card.

Trim: 2 by 3½ inches
Stock: speckletone cover, spruce
Type: old-fashioned serif computer type
Printing: one color: black
Finish: hand-colored

Fascinated by all things Italian, she doodled, then twisted her sketches together into a miniature grapevine design. Her husband scanned the sketch onto a computer and experimented with layouts and font combinations for the art and lettering. All elements were enlarged, reduced, or shaped into various sizes and forms until the right combination appeared on the screen. In the final product, the type for the logo was compressed enough to fit within the curve of the underlying vine. Paula's name and telephone number were balanced and justified beneath the logotype, and a small decorative bullet and italic type were chosen to highlight the company description.

With as many copies of the computer-printed design as she could squeeze onto an 8½ by 11 sheet of paper, Paula went to a local copy shop. For pennies a page, the designs were photocopied onto a heavy, dark-colored stock chosen to offset her handpainted metallic gold "gilding," yet light enough to showcase the delicate violet and apple-green inks. A slight pink in the paper contrasts with the green leaves and makes them strikingly visible. The cards were then cut out from the photocopied sheet. A bit of handpainting and the calling card was ready to go.

A GLOSSARY OF DESIGN TERMS

Bleed — *the part of an image extending beyond the trim of a page. This technique necessitates exact cutting.*

Blind embossing — *relief or raised printing without the use of foil or ink.*

Boldface — *a heavier version of plain type; type with a heavy, dense appearance.*

Book fold — *the folding of a card along its side similar to the binding of a book.*

Bullet — *a dot, which can be any size or shape, used as a decorative or organizing device.*

Caps and small caps — *type consisting of two sizes of capital letters, the small caps being the same size as the body of lowercase letters.*

Centered — *lines of type centered on a central axis.*

Characters — *individual letters, numerals, and punctuation marks.*

Chromolithography — *a nineteenth-century stone lithographic printing method designed to allow printing in several colors.*

Column width — *the measurement from the left to the right side of a group of lines of type.*

Comp — *a tight rendering of a layout or design accurately indicating the relationships among all elements.*

Condensed — *a narrower version of the normal width of a typeface.*

Copy — *all artwork to be printed: type, photographs, and illustrations.*

Die — *the stamp of an image on the surface of a plate used for impressing a design.*

Die-cutting — *cutting paper, card, or board to a particular shape with a metal die.*

Dingbat — *an ornamental piece of type for borders, separators, or decorations.*

Embossing — *relief or raised designs on paper, cloth, or leather.*

Engraving — *printing of art or lettering from an etched plate or block; the final print produced by this method.*

Expanded — *a wider version of the normal width of a typeface.*

Finish — *the surface (i.e. matte or glossy) given to paper during manufacturing.*

Flat-color printing — *the printing of custom matched colors and also varying shades of black to produce the final effect. Flat-color is used primarily for simple text and illustrations.*

Flush — *type that is aligned on one side (i.e. flush left or flush right).*

Foil — *an extremely thin, flexible metal used for stamping letters or designs on a surface.*

Foil-stamping — *impressing a surface with decorative foil, using pressure and heat.*

Font — *one size and design of a given typeface, including caps and lower case letters, accented characters, punctuation, bullets, and symbols.*

Four color process — *a method of printing color images by separating them into the four process colors and assigning each color its own plate. When the plates print over one another they simulate all the colors of the original art. Used primarily for printing color photography.*

Full-bleed — *an image extending beyond the trim on all sides of a page.*

Glossy — *a type of paper finish with a shiny appearance.*

Justified type — *lines of type that are aligned on both the right and left margins.*

Layout — *an outline or sketch which gives the overall view of a printed page in order to visualize type and artwork together.*

Letter spacing — *the space between individual letters.*

Line spacing — *the space measured from the baseline of one line of type to the next; also known as leading.*

Lithography — *a particular type of planographic printing in which the surface of the printing plate is flat. The image areas are separated from non-image areas by a chemical process similar to the principle of oil/water repulsion.*

Logotype — *artwork, words, or several letters treated as one unit.*

Matte — *a dull paper finish achieved by applying a clay coating.*

Measure — *the length of a line of type usually expressed in picas.*

Mechanical — *all the elements of camera-ready-copy including illustrations, photos, and printer's instructions ready to be reproduced by a printer. The printer translates mechanicals onto films from which the printing plates are made.*

Plate — *a surface treated to carry an image. Plates are made of rubber, synthetic rubber, plastic, and (most commonly) metal.*

PMS — *the Pantone Matching System. A trade name for a system of color matching in designer's materials such as inks, papers, and marker pens.*

Point — *the standard unit of type size.*

Process colors — *the four primary colors used in Four-Color Process printing: cyan, yellow, magenta, and black.*

Register — *the correct positioning of one color over another in color printing.*

Reverse type — *white or light colored type within a dark background. The background color is actually printed on top of paper or lighter ink to form the image. Reverse type is also known as drop out type.*

Rules — *lines printed for decoration or organization; also typographic elements whose thickness is specified in points.*

Sans Serif — *type without serifs.*

Serifs — *the small terminal strokes, or feet, at the end of the main strokes of letters.*

Stock — *the printer's term for the material onto which an image is printed: paper, board, foil, etc.*

Tent fold — *the folding of a card in half across the top so that it stands like a tent.*

Trim — *to cut the printed piece out of a larger piece of stock after printing; the final proportions of the printed piece.*

Typeface — *any number of named styles of type such as Caslon, Garamond, or Zapf.*

CREDITS

8: Photograph by John E. Kane

10-19: From the collection of Raymond Rieser

20-21: From the collection of Marlene Harris

22: Twigs card designed by Cheryl Lewin

25: A Touch of Ivy card designed by Goulet/Grann Art Direction

26: Judith Cheng card designed by Judith Cheng

27: Mary Polityka Bush card designed by Mary Polityka Bush and Marsha A. Isley

28-29: M. Balin Interior Art card designed by Marna Balin

30: Michèle card designed by James Ronson

31: Hat & the Heart card designed by Diane Glenn

32: Poupi La Poupée card designed by Denise Landriault

33: Sharon Brown card designed by Sharon Brown

34: Bunnies by the Bay card designed by Kristine Andersen

35: The Jenny Wren Press card designed by Tasha Tudor

36: Granny-Made card designed by Eric Rosenberg and Michelle Kolb

37: Renaissance Buttons card designed by Roosje Penfold

Pulled Out a Plum card designed by Carol Hudson-Fitzsimmons

38: Forget-Me-Nots Design card designed by Krista Ingalls

39: Tail of the Yak card designed by Lauren Allard

40-41: Pentimento card designed by Anne Marie Scarano

42: Love Laces card designed by Laurinda Stockwell

43: The Piccadilly Collection card designed by W.A. Buening & Co. and Judith Q. Stewart

Plumelle at Plumquin Ltd. card designed by Teri Scheinzeit

44: Patches etc. card designed by Jael Watkins

45: Helen Lloyd card designed by Douglas Lloyd

Seams To Be card designed by LN Vaillancourt

46: Andrea Stieff card designed by Susanna Steiff

47: The Tinker's Daughter Landscaping card designed by Catherine Colwell Stimson

48: Three Lives & Company Ltd. card designed by Susanna Kelly and Jenny Feder

49: Hudson Street Papers card designed by Lesia Eutsler and Josh Gosfield

50: Thomas Whitehill card designed by Thomas Whitehill

52: Hollyhock card designed by Michael Brock Designs

54: Angels Workshop card designed by Nan Hadala

Wendy Christensen card designed by Wendy Christensen

55: Cynthia Petters card designed by Cynthia Petters

56: Private Gardener card designed by Victoria Vonier

57: Repeat Performance card designed by Jim Heimann

Gael Paints card designed by Gael Tynefield

58: Petals card designed by Nicholas Clemens

Patricia Melville card designed by Patricia Melville

59: Plumbush card designed by Elena Erber and Vivian Wadlin

60: Props card designed by Scott McKowen

61: Élan card designed by Brian Toel and Elizabeth Toel

Pugh Design card designed by Peggy Pugh

62: Shoofly card designed by Barbara Ensor

63: Savoy card designed by Salestrom and Zingg Inc.

64: Patina Millinery card designed by Jodi Bentsen and Katrin Noon

65: Emerald Forest Entertainment card designed by Claudia Laub, Marla McNally; art by Linda Blum-Huntington, and Michael Christman

Arcadia card designed by Arcadia

66: Cats Cradle card designed by Patricia Melville

67: It's About Thyme card designed by Kimberly Childers

68: Julia Boston card designed by Julia Boston

69: Alice Simpson card designed by Alice Simpson

70: Janet McCaffery card designed by Barry Disman

71: Friends card designed by Bob Thomas

72: Jacqui Morgan card designed by Jacqui Morgan

73: Bell'occhio card designed by Jody Hanson

74: Old Waverly card designed by Donna Beth Joy Shapiro

75: Capability Brown card designed by Gerald Reis

76: Ginny Joyner card designed by Ginny Joyner

77: Trillium card designed by Kathryn Hettinga

78: Ŝuzy's Searsport Boutique card designed by Rosalie Idall and Susan Fernau

79: Love Gifts card designed by Steven and Kim Elowe

80: Secret Garden card designed by Sindy Kelley

81: Buttons & Beyond card designed by Paula Zonan-Goldberg

82: Growing Graphics card designed by Nancee McDonell

83: Terra Cotta card designed by Darren Waterston

89: Dorothy Wilson Caterers Card designed by (?Paradox!)

91: A Gilded Vine card designed by Paula Arndt-Berger and David Berger

ACKNOWLEDGMENTS

The editors would like to thank all those who have contributed their cards to *Victoria's* calling card column and to this book. Special thanks is given to Janet Harrington and Colleen Rogan of *Victoria*, who each month survey the cards collected and make the selections of the ones to appear in the magazine's column. The importance of their role, beside picking cards for a special season or occasion, is their absolute dedication to the design quality of each card. It is because of their high standards that this is a unique collection.